How T

*Master the Basics of S   ....y und
Easily - The Ultimate Beginners Guide to
Skiing*

Contents

Introduction

I want to thank you for choosing to read "How to Ski - Master The Basics Of Skiing Quickly And Easily - The Ultimate Beginners Guide To Skiing." This book has been designed with total beginners in mind and I guess that you are a beginner, we have all been there and although skiing may look daunting to begin with it, it is one of the most rewarding forms of sport and something that can be enjoyed by all of the family at the same time.

Obviously it goes without saying that skiing is dangerous and therefore it is vital that you take heed and learn the basics from scratch even before you take your first lesson and I have drawn a lot of inspiration from my own experiences as a beginner to the sport of skiing. I can openly admit that I was petrified when I first took to the slopes, however this was in a good way and as my confidence grew so did my ability on my skis. Although you obviously need to be able to stand on skis and go through all of the other motions, confidence is the one thing that will enhance your progression and skiing prowess tenfold. However bearing this in mind it is important that you do not become overconfident as this is a sure fire way to injury.

It does take time to learn to ski and it is vital that you take the time and don't try to run before you can walk! Depending on where you live, if you are planning a skiing trip in the future and you have never skied before a really useful trip would be to your nearest indoor skiing facility as this way you can master the basics and be ready to start on your lessons and beginners trails almost as soon as you arrive on your holiday destination.

I won't delay you further, except to wish you the best of luck in your new pursuit and above all else be sure to enjoy yourself safely and responsibly.

Chapter 1 – The Origins of Skiing

For thousands of years before skiing was recognized as a sport it was used as a means to get across snowy ground. There are a number of different beliefs to when and where skiing was first uncovered, with many believing that the oldest skis are those that were found in Moscow that are assumed to be about 8,000 years old. There were also skis found in Sweden which are believed to date back as far as 3,200 BC. However, regardless of these beliefs it was 1933 in Norway where the first rock carvings were found and these depicted men using skis. Further carvings have been uncovered in other parts of the country with the last one being uncovered in 2001.

To date there have been more than 200 prehistoric skis discovered in various parts of the world most predominately in the marshy terrains of Sweden, Russia and Norway. These skis are currently undergoing carbon dating to ensure that any tests results are accurate as past testing has proved to be unreliable.

There are references to skiing that can be found in Norse mythology when the gods and goddesses were said to have hunted using skis. There are also texts which refer to Onduris, the goddess of skiing as a name accredited to the finest skier of all the gods.

Currently, cross country races are still held regularly in Norway and Sweden as a celebration of the early accounts of skiing as part of medieval life. Until the 1700s, skis were designed for gliding over flat surfaces and as the art of skiing became more popular and refined skis began to be used not just for practical purposes but also for sport. It was at this time that people began downhill skiing using jumps for recreational purposes as opposed to just logistical reasons. As original skis were not designed or made for jumping or downhill skiing a new era for skiing began.

The very first Birkebeiner Run took place in Norway in 1932. The ski run is believed to date back to 1205 AD, and the event occurs annually to date and is to commemorate this well-known run, with the only difference today being that the event now incorporates a combination of mountain bike racing and cross country skiing with both elements requiring the contestants to carry a backpack that weights 3.5kg.

After World War 11 skiing increased even more in popularity and by the 1950s skis began to be made from metal as opposed to the original wooden models that only had metal edges. It was also at this point that quick release bindings were invented to reduce the chance of injury and this time also saw the introduction of lightweight poles which led to vast changes in the way that turns were executed on the slopes. It wasn't long after this that American ski resorts began to offer lifts and hotel services, soon after snow making machines and slope climbing units came into force.

Whilst skiing has evolved tenfold in every aspect and is a great deal safer than ever before it is still as exciting as ever.

Chapter 2 – Ski Equipment

Once you have made the choice to take up skiing there are various essential pieces of clothing and equipment that are necessary. For this reason this chapter will look at all of these essentials in detail.

Ski jacket

It is important to realize that when you purchase a ski jacket this involves far more than simply buying an item of clothing that is comfortable and stylish. Whilst it is important to choose a jacket that suits your sense of style and personality it is far more important that the jacket also offers a number of practical features.

Probably the most important feature is a jacket that is waterproof or has a water resistant outer shell. After all there will be nothing worse than being weighed down by a water logged jacket whilst on the slopes. Nearly all ski jackets nowadays are designed with waterproofing.

To achieve flexibility from your ski jacket you may want to look to purchase a jacket that has a removable lining as this will make your jacket suitable for both cold and hot weather. The lining should be breathable as this allows any moisture and or body heat to escape. Ideally the jacket will have some strategically placed air vents inclusive of zippers so that you can close the vents in the colder weather.

Skiing requires you to be able to wear a number of layers therefore it is advised to choose a jacket that is one size larger than you would normally wear. It is also a good idea to try the jacket on over a few layers before you purchase as this will give you a good sense of how your jacket will feel when you hit the slopes.

Once incredibly convenient feature that is suggested in a ski jacket yet commonly overlooked are a variety of zippered pockets. These pockets make an excellent place for keeping items such as keys, money etc. It is important that you choose good quality zippers as the last thing that you want is to end up struggling to open or close the pockets when on the top of a mountain. Be sure to try the zippers out to ensure that they operate smoothly and they do not become snagged in the fabric of your jacket.

It is not essential that your ski jacket has a hood as you will more than likely be wearing a ski hat to keep you warm. A hood is definitely useful though particularly if you find yourself in the middle of a snowstorm as a hood will provide you with added protection from the snow and the wind.

Choosing your helmet

There are two vital reasons for you to take extra care and protect your head when you are skiing.

Firstly wearing a helmet will dramatically reduce the chances of you suffering from any injuries and or serious damage to your head. Secondly a helmet will protect you from the cold by keeping your head warm. It is important to choose a suitable helmet before taking to the slopes.

Ski helmets are entirely different to cycling helmets although they look reasonably similar. Ski helmets are designed specifically to protect the user from the hazards that are typically associated with skiing.

The following components and features are most important to look for when you choose your ski helmet:

Resistant to impact

Whichever helmet you use, a hard outer is required that is capable of absorbing shock, strong impact and is also scratch resistant. The design of the helmet should be able to withstand shock evenly and in the event of an accident there is no chance of intense pressure in any single part of your head. The helmet should also be appropriately lined to protect from serious brain injuries, and a good liner which compresses in the event of an accident to provide maximum protection and then expands unaided. If you are unlucky and have a fall and the lining remains compressed it is time for a new one.

Ventilation

It is important that you helmet has adequate ventilation. You are likely to have a considerable build-up of moisture on both your head and face when you ski, and this presence of moisture will make wearing your helmet uncomfortable and could even become a distraction. This is why it is so important for your helmet to have adequate vents for proper inflow and outflow of air.

Fitting

It is imperative that you helmet fits correctly, and there should be no gap between the top of your ski goggles and your helmet. Your helmet must protect your forehead therefore it should sit right above your ski goggles and about an inch from your eyebrows. Your helmet should also allow you to use interior pads to ensure the perfect fit.

Apart from these three vital components there are several other things that you should so and precautions that you can take to minimize the likelihood of an injury, and wearing the right helmet will be a great deal of help should you end up in a precarious situation.

Ski boots

In order to ensure you get the right ski boots it is important that you understand what a boot fitting entails. To begin with fitting for ski boots is not just about choosing the color, graphics and getting someone to measure your foot. All that this kind of fitting will give you is pain!

The first thing that you should do when going for your ski boot fitting is adequate time and on average you need to allow at least half an hour for this process however some fittings can take as long as two hours if you have particularly requirements. The following details what a general boot fitting will entail:

Talk about it

The sign of a good fitter is one who will sit down with you and spend a few minutes just talking through your requirements. They should ask about your skiing style and whether you have any issues with your lower back, legs, knees or any other part of your body. Usually it is your feet that have to cope with most things and it can take very little for any problem to go from your feet to other parts of your body. A good fitter will not proceed to the next step until they have gauged a basic understanding of your requirements.

Analyze

A good fitter will next take a few minutes to analyze your feet before they begin with the actual fitting. They will more than likely use a Podoscope, this piece of equipment has a pale blue light which is fired under your feet so that you can see what is going on. There are fitters that may also use a thermal plate to draw the outline of your foot. This allows the fitter to observe your stance and see whether you are canting or bowing in your legs, particularly with relation to your knees and hips. From these observations, the fitter can form a profile of your feet along with the measurements of your feet's width and length, allowing the fitter to determine the volume of ski boots that need to be fitted.

Fitting

Finally you may need to try on a few pairs of boots so that the fitter can find the ones that are best suited to your foot profile and personal requirements. Once the right pair is identified the fitter will make the insoles specifically designed for your feet based upon the results from the first two steps. The insoles are then heated up and moulded. Then you have to try the boots on and walk around for a few minutes to see if they feel comfortable enough. If at this point there are any issues identified the boots will be taken to the workshops for the necessary adjustments to be made and the fitter will then refit, recheck and repeat this step as necessary.

It is vital that you do not choose your ski boots simply based on brand and colour alone, and it is imperative that you devote enough time to proper boot fitting. By having boots that fit properly you are not only making sure that you are comfortable but it will also improve your overall skiing performance.

Goggles

You will probably already know how important it is to wear the proper gear when you take to the slopes. For this reason, you are probably already careful about wearing your pants and ski helmet when you go out, but if you are like so many people you probably often take for granted the importance of ski goggles. Although you may not realize it is extremely important that you wear the right ski goggles as these can make a lot of difference in your performance as well as your total overall experience. This is particularly true since lens technologies are so much more advanced and now range from photo chromic lenses to interchangeable lenses. Do not begin to despair though as it is easy enough to find suitable ski goggles for all manner of weather conditions. There are a number of things you need to take into consideration when you shop for a pair of ski goggles.

One of the things that the majority of skiers find very challenging is the task of identifying a white object when it is lying on the equally white snow. The task of adjusting to visual changes in fast paced and snow-covered environment can be just as challenging. These are instances where having the right pair of ski goggles will come in very handy.

Goggles are offered in a wide variety of colours that help to increase contrast and improve visibility as well as provide depth perception particularly when you are faced with changing lighting conditions. It is important to remember that different lens tints are suitable for different lighting. Orange tints are perfect for skiing in sunny weather conditions whilst amber and gold are advisable when skiing in moderate lighting conditions. Amber and gold are the best options for skiing in low to moderate lighting whilst rose and yellow are perfect for overcast days.

Ski goggles do not only benefit you by helping you to identify objects in the slopes snowy landscape but you should note that your eyes can be harmed by overexposure to UV rays even on the most cloudy of days. When you are in high altitude areas such as a ski resort, the intensity of the UV rays is higher than usual and you are likely to suffer from a condition that is referred to as snow blindness. When you take this into consideration coupled with the wide expanse of snow you encounter when skiing, you will understand the severity of the serious risk of harming your eyes. Research has shown that snow has the ability to reflect up to 80% of the UV radiation that it encounters therefore just imagine what it can do if it gets reflected directly into your eyes, and this is why it is vital for you to always wear quality ski goggles whilst on a skiing adventure.

There are a number of manufacturers that have also produced ski goggles equipped with a fog dissipation feature to help provide you with a clear view of your surroundings even when you encounter extreme conditions.

It is also important that your ski goggles are compatible with your ski helmet and this is not only to avoid discomfort but also as it can be a distraction whilst you ski. You may want to buy your goggles and helmet at the same time so that you can try them out together.

Skis

Every skiing enthusiast has to go through the task of buying their first pair of skis. For those just starting out they are actually quite lucky because they can make use of the wealth of information about skis which is offered online, in magazines and even consult with friends that may have been skiing for some time. Buying a pair of skis is a very large investment, but it can provide amazing payback provided that you make the right choice. The most obvious advantage of having your own skis is that you won't have to waste time waiting your turn in ski rental queues.

The following will provide you with enough knowledge to choose the right pair of skis:

Types of skis

The first thing you need to do to get the right pair of skis is to determine what type of skier you are, as well as the type of skier you hope to become. This is because there are different types of skis that suit different types of skiers these are as follows:

Piste skis

As the name implies, these skis are best suited for skiing on piste and in good snow conditions. The skis are excellent carvers and there are models that use the same technology as used in the racing scene. The disadvantage though is that you're likely to struggle of they go off piste when skiing in less than perfect conditions.

All-mountain skis

These skis allow you to ski in various snow conditions, regardless of whether the snow is slushy or icy and they will perform better than piste skis. The disadvantage of all mountain skis is that they have a tendency to lose a bit of carving ability unless you choose to buy higher end models that are equipped with the latest technology for maintaining carving ability.

Back-country skis

This type of ski is perfect for hiking all over the mountains, they are typically versatile enough to use out of bounds and much lighter than other skis meaning that they are far easier to carry uphill. These skis do not come with their own bindings therefore you have to choose the appropriate bindings in accordance to your needs.

Off-piste skis

These skis are ideal for skiing in off-piste conditions and on powder snow. Typically they are far wider and more forgiving allowing the user to feel more in the powder whilst also allowing for the absorption of impact during jump and landings.

Length

Once you have determined the type of skis need, the next thing to do is determine the right ski length for your needs. The most important factors when choosing a length for your skis are your height, weight and skiing ability. Generally the skis will be too short if they reach below the tip of your nose and if when held upright they are taller than you they are too long. There are exceptions to this rule; this is why you need to take your weight and ability into consideration. The ski store will have a sizing guide that will help you to choose the right ski length for you.

Chapter 3 – Indoor Skiing

Skiing is a topic of conversation that makes many people automatically think it of an outdoor sport however skiing is a sport that can not only be enjoyed during winter when there are blankets of snow covering the mountains. Although this might have been the case in the past, due to human ingenuity it is now possible to ski indoors whenever you wish. There are now a number of outdoor and indoor ski facilities which means that this is a sport that can be enjoyed all year round.

This may be the first time that you have become aware of indoor skiing and you may be wondering why you should try it instead of going directly to the real thing. The truth about indoor skiing is that there really are not that many differences when compared to outdoor skiing. After all you still get to ski down a slope and feel the cold from the snowy ground. The biggest difference is probably that the snow in this case is produced by machines rather than nature, but the good news is that this artificial snow cannot be considered inferior in any way to natural snow. A number of indoor ski facilities are designed so professionally that they are now even used in official competitions.

There are no quality issues related to indoor skiing but the significant advantage of trying indoor skiing is that it is ideal for those that have never skied before. It is important to remember skiing can be a very dangerous activity primarily because you will be going down a mountain slope at a very quick pace. As the indoor facilities are far more forgiving than outdoor slopes it is far easier and safer for you to learn to ski indoors due to the surfaces of the indoor slopes being specifically designed to absorb falls more effectively. Indoor slopes are also understandably more predictable than outdoor slopes and you will know exactly what you are dealing with.

There are obvious reasons while why many outdoor ski resorts are only open during the winter, but because they are self-maintained indoor skiing facilities can be opened all year round meaning the skiing experience can be enjoyed even during hot summer months. There are many professional skiers who use indoor facilities to train for the sport all year round.

As a beginner you can use indoor skiing facilities to master the basic skiing techniques, and then when the time comes to hit the slopes you will start with confidence. There are numerous reasons why adrenaline junkies become hooked on indoor skiing and this is because it allows them to enjoy the thrill of the skiing experience at any time whilst being far safer, therefore indoor skiing can indeed be the best precursor to the real thing. Anyone that is learning to ski should practice in safety to gain confidence in their skills before they hit the outdoor slopes.

Chapter 4 – Fitness Training for Skiing

Skiing is an extremely strenuous activity when being undertaken for recreational purposes, even more so when you undertake skiing as a competitive sport regardless of the variation that you choose. For this reason it is important that you work hard to ensure you are in good enough shape to meet the physical demands that this sport requires in terms of balance, speed and agility. It is for this reason that it is so important for you to engage in ski fitness training.

In an ideal situation you will start you ski fitness program at least 8 weeks prior to stepping foot onto the slopes. The plan should be to build your muscular strength and development maximum endurance particularly in your legs. In the same way that you would any other fitness training program you need to remember to warm up properly before you begin the exercise components of your training.

During your warm up session you should include gentle stretching as this will sufficiently prepare your body for the intense activity that follows. As this type of warm up stimulates your blood circulation and initiates the secretion of bodily fluids which will help to feed your muscles and lubricate your joints. You should begin to stretch from the top of the body and then slowly work downwards without rushing and it should take you about 15 minutes to complete your stretches completely. Once the stretching session is complete you would be advised to spend 20 minutes on a treadmill at a pace that is somewhere between a fast walk and slow jog. Basic cardio training like this will strengthen your heart and will help to lower your bad cholesterol levels whilst also improving your overall lung function at the same time.

Ski fitness training must simulate the actual type and extent of physical activity involved with skiing as closely as possible and it is therefore a good idea to consider including exercises such as using a skipping rope in your ski fitness training program, this is because this type of exercise will not only improve your blood circulation but also sufficiently condition your knees into the constant bending. At the same time it helps you to develop strength and endurance in your fine muscles. Skipping is a lot faster than jogging and as so it effectively exercises your fast muscle fibres allowing which allow your legs to respond quickly to the undulating conditions that you will encounter on a ski slope.

Finally it is advisable to include weight training in your ski fitness program. When you incorporate weight training focus on lower intensity with high repetitions as your aim is to condition your muscles and develop endurance rather than to build up bulk. It is best to use free weights instead of fixed weights as this allows you to gain a better balance and coordination is your core strength increases, which will then stabilize your trunk and spine. By following these tips you will be well on your way towards improving your skiing skills and avoiding serious injuries.

Obviously, it is also very important that you reinforce your fitness training with proper nutrition and although there isn't a specific diet that is recommended for skiers, if you are in any doubt it is probably best to consult a professional nutritionist who will be able to assist you in developing the most suitable nutrition plan to complement your ski fitness training.

Chapter 5 – Beginners' Basic Skiing Tips

Understandably the task of learning how to ski may seem rather daunting however you shouldn't be discouraged by this. Skiing can be an excellent sport to learn as it's a lot of fun, it's exhilarating and helps you to burn a lot of calories and skiing requires skill and eventually will take you to some of the world's best mountain locations.

One of the keys to learning how to ski is your equipment, although you don't have to spend a fortune it is ill-advised to go with the cheapest equipment you can find, as doing so could make it far more difficult and much less fun for you to learn the sport. It is most important that you buy a ski hat of decent quality, a good pair of ski gloves and scarf, plus ski socks and thermal pants. To begin with you can rent ski boots, skis and poles at the ski resort. Once fully equipped you are ready to learn the basics of skiing.

Standing on skis

The most obvious thing and first thing you need to do when learning to ski is to learn how to stand with your skis on. When you try to get off the ground after putting on your skis you must make sure that you are facing the side of the slope rather than downhill, as this will avoid you ending up going down the slope a whole lot sooner than you expected.

Stance

This point may seem obvious to those who have skied before or watched many skiing events, however many people are unaware that you need to bend your knees and lean slightly forwards. Life on the slopes will be far much harder if you fail to do this.

Snowplough

Once you can stand comfortably and take the proper stance, it is time to start moving downhill. Towards the end, you will need to keep your knees bent and then push your weight forward as you face downhill. When you want to stop, point your toes in and push your heels slightly outwards and if you happen to cross your skis simply lift the top ski up with your foot and try the manoeuvre again. If at any point panic overtakes and you really want to stop just sit down.

Turning

When you want to make a turn, turn your feet towards your desired direction and whilst this may sound easy, it actually takes a little bit of practice. This can easily be done in the snowplough position and then you can proceed to parallel turns once you are confident enough. You need to face the direction you want to go without looking at your skis as this may make you lose track of the position on the slope. It is important to remember that a huge part of skiing is confidence; you need to know your limits and ensure safety at all time, however remain confident in your skiing ability. If you lose confidence and start to panic this is when you are more likely to fall and that is something you do not want to happen.

Chapter 6 – Safety

For those that have never engaged in winter sports they will probably be wondering if there's any difference between snowboarding and skiing. Although these two activities are practically the same, apart from the fact that skiers use skis and snowboarders use snowboards. When it comes to the task of ensuring your safety there are a world of difference between these two outdoor activities. There are similarities such as the fact that skiers and snowboarders are both required to wear helmets and only ski or snowboard within the limits of their abilities. In the same vein as any other sport, the basic rule is to always stay alert, be attentive and be prepared.

Winter sports such as skiing have grown in popularity over the recent years and as the number of people participating in the sports continues to increase the number of injury cases are also on the increase.

The most common type of injury associated with skiing is a head injury, and it is these injuries that account for half of the cases of death associated with winter sports. The second most common type of injury that is suffered by skiers all over the world is wrist injuries. Every skiing season sees approximately 10,000 incidents of fractured wrists in northern America alone. The best way to avoid any form of injury that can be caused by skiing is to take lessons from a professional. During these lessons you will be taught about the intricacies of skiing which include the art of falling with your hands held in a fist position.

Research that was undertaken shows that the use of protective gear such as helmets, ski gloves, wrist guards and the like can reduce the risk of injury by as much as 40%.

The following tips are designed to offer advice on how you can avoid wrist injuries:

1. Take ski lessons from an experienced ski coach, a good coach will not only teach you how to ski but also how to board and fall without hurting yourself.

2. In the case where you fall forwards, it is important to fall on your fore arms rather than your hands and if you fall backwards you should try to let your bottom take the brunt of the fall and refrain at all times from trying to protect yourself with your hands.

3. Every time you fall, be sure to hold your hands in a fist instead of opening them as this will offer a bit of support and prevent your fingers from splaying out. Good ski gloves also come in handy in these instances as these will cushion your hands and reduce the risk of injury; some ski gloves are even equipped with built-in wrist guards.

4. Strive to use your forearms so that your wrists are kept stable and prevented from hyper extension.

5. Always put your forearms down to protect your face from hitting the ground.

6. Be sure to use the right ski equipment at all times and ensure that your ski gloves, tailbone pads, wrist guards, knee pads, elbow pads, helmet etc. all fit properly and are all of good quality. You might want to consider buying a combination pack or ski gear set as this could be the best way to take advantage of some great discounts on quality items.

7. Keep yourself in shape at all times, skiing is one sport that requires much in terms of physical fitness and you will surely be able to enjoy it far more if you are in good shape.

Chapter 7 – Improve Your Balance

One of the key components to becoming a good skier is balance; therefore improving your balance is an excellent way to improve your overall performance when you hit the slopes. Having good balance also increases your confidence in your own skiing abilities and as you know skiing is foremost about confidence.

An extremely good way to improve your balance is by engaging in exercises that enhance your total muscle strength, this is particularly important with skiing as it is a physically demanding sport.

The following are a few of the balance exercises that you may want to look to incorporate into your ski fitness training routine:

Single leg deadlifts

Single leg deadlifts will see you strengthening your glutes, hamstrings and the lower back whilst also improving your balance. It is important when you execute this exercise that you try to think of lifting with your glutes instead of pulling through your back as this will see you achieve better results.

Single leg split squats

The second exercise that you should consider incorporating in your workout routine works to target your hamstrings, quads and glutes and this is also an excellent exercise for improving core strength. Be sure to maintain an upright position throughout the movements when you perform this exercise as doing so will help prevent the development of lower back pain and also make sure that you're targeting the right muscle groups.

Lateral raise on one leg

This final exercise works to strengthen your shoulder muscles, and whilst you may not think this has a lot to do with balance, working your shoulders whilst standing on one leg boosts your balance very effectively.

In order to maintain a good muscular balance, you need to make sure you perform the exercise in an equal number of repetitions for both sides; a good starting point is two sets of 10 to 15 repetitions on both sides.

Whilst there are a number of other exercises, these are just three of the best that can effectively improve your balance and subsequently improve your skiing performance as well.

It is important to remember your ability to ski begins and ends with your ability to maintain good balance when your skis on, and this is why it's so important to start incorporating these exercises into your ski fitness training sessions as soon as possible and it won't be long before you see significant results. For those considering competing in skiing events it is very important that they constantly work on improving their balance, and as the balance improves, they will find that they have more control of their movements and skiing which will result in more confidence when it is time to hit the slopes.

Once you have mastered your balance who knows you may even grow confident enough to start learning tricks, the likes of which are essential in most skiing competitions. Why wait? The sooner you start working on these exercises the sooner you will see your balance improving and there is no doubt that you will thank yourself in the long run.

Chapter 8 – Improve Your Core Agility

In your quest to become a good skier it is important that you continue to work on your ski fitness training routines. These routines are excellent ways of boosting your performance and also helping you to avoid possible injuries. It is important to remember that skiing can be very physically demanding and you could be putting yourself at risk of getting injured in a number of ways. This is why it is so important for you to make sure you are in good enough shape to withstand the visit of physical demands that skiing commands.

The good thing with regards to ski fitness training workouts is that they do not take up too much time and they do have a huge influence on the level of your skiing skills. One particular element of your physical fitness that you will need to address with your training routine is that of your core strength. It is vital that you engage regularly in exercises as this is essential to keeping injury free when you hit the slopes.

Here are some of the best exercises that you can undertake to improve your core agility and strength:

Lying leg raise with a twist

The first exercises ideal for targeting your oblique muscles as well as your upper and lower abdominals. This exercise will also help improve your muscular endurance. To perform this exercise you need to lift your legs straight out 90° and then slowly shift them to the side as far down as you can go while still maintaining total control over the movement pattern. When you have lowered your legs to their total limits, reverse the direction and repeat the movement on the other side.

Pike on a ball

This second exercises is also an excellent exercise for improving agility as it requires you to use the exercise ball. This exercise will help to improve your shoulder strength. When you are ready to perform this exercise you need to place your feet on the exercise ball and your hands on the floor beneath you, contracting your abdominal muscles so that you form an inverted V shape. Hold the position for a second and then straight back out into your full position, rest briefly and repeat the exercise 5 to 8 times.

Reverse crunch

The final exercise suggested is ideal for strengthening your lower abdominals and making sure that you can maintain constant tension in your core whilst you ski. To perform this exercise you need to lie flat on the floor with your legs bent and then pull your legs into your chest as hard as possible, pause briefly, and reverse the movement pattern and this completes one repetition. Start by dong 10 to 12 repetitions, before resting and then repeating the entire exercise.

By adding these three exercises into your ski fitness training routine you will surely notice significant core strengthening benefits which will help reduce your chances of getting sidelined due to injury. For those serious about building a career in competitive skiing it is vital that they are serious about getting into shape for the sport. Skiing may look easy; however it is a tough sport unless you are fit enough.

Chapter 9 – Basic Skiing

When asked about skiing many people conjure up ideas of pure white snow, hot chocolates complete with fluffy marshmallows, and whilst this idyllic is true it is very important that you remember that skiing is not for the fainthearted and definitely no walk in the park.

Skiing is thrilling and will satiate anyone's need for an adrenaline hit. For those that have always wanted to ski but not yet had the opportunity this chapter is designed to help you get started. Bear in mind that although this article covers the basics of downhill skiing there is no substitute for real lessons, therefore I urge you to read this, then go and enroll in some lessons to begin your snowy adventures.

The rules of the slopes

It is vital that you learn how to distinguish the difficult of the various trails. You can tell how difficult a trail is by the symbol that is used on the trail marker or ski map. For example in Northern America trail difficulties are shown as below:

Green circle – this indicates an easy, beginners trail and these are trails that are not too fast have few obstacles and are relatively short.

Blue square – this indicates an intermediate trail and may contain some obstacles and steeper gradients and these trails should not be attempted until the easier trails are mastered.

Black diamond – this is used to indicate a difficult trail that will contain obstacles, small snow hills and a steep gradient with a narrow way down. These trails should not be tried by inexperienced skiers, and whilst you may feel that you are ready the chances are that you will not be. Many injuries have occurred from those that have attempted this type of trail too early.

Double black diamond or a black diamond complete with exclamation mark – this indicates a trail which is only suitable for extremely good skiers and should not be attempted by anyone unless they are accomplished and totally happy with all other types of trails. Always double check these trails and be aware that if they have EX in the middle this indicates an expert only trail and as so are purely for experts. These slopes are also very avalanche-prone.

Trail notes

When looking at the difficulty ratings of trails it is important to note that each trail can only be compared to another one at the same resort. In other words, a trail that is marked with the Blue Square at one resort may be more challenging than a trail marked with black diamond at another. It is for this reason when you are skiing at a new resort you should always begin with a green man and work your way up even if you are very accomplished skier.

It is important you know has the right of way on the slate. People ahead if you in other words down the slope you have the right of way. You are responsible to make sure that you avoid them even if they fall immediately in front of you. At, because of this it is best to keep a fair amount of distance between you and the skier or snowboarder in front.

It is important to always stay in control when on the slate and it is your responsibility to know what speed and sleep difficulty you can handle. In other words do not go on a black diamond simply because you think you're a natural born skier when you actually haven't skied before. If you do decide to behave in this way you run the risk of causing serious injury or even killing another skier or yourself if you crash.

It is important that you remember not to stop if you cannot be seen from above and whilst it is common to stop you catch your breath on the slave it is extremely dangerous to stop if you would obstruct the trail or cannot be seen by those coming down the trail. If you do feel the need to stop always try to stop at the top of the next section of the slave which is visible from above that pull over to the side of the trail.

Putting on your skis

If you are renting your boots with us the attendant to help you figure out which beat is best for you as you need to find the right size and adjust the tightness. When you are at rest your foot should not be compressed however you do want it to immobile, your foot should not press against the front of the boot when you bend your knees to point your shins slightly forward at the angle of the boot. The top of the boot needs to be snug around your ankle. It is far easier to walk in ski boots by taking long steps and smoothly rolling this dispute forward heel to toe with your lower leg straight as it passes over your body. With your boots in place take your poles and skis under your arm until you reach the snow. The edges of the skis can be sharp or they may have rough places therefore always wear gloves to carry them.

Separate your skis as they might be locked together bottom to bottom by a clip which extends from the bindings past the flat sides. This is to keep your skis from sliding away when they come away from your boots if you fall; this is so that your knees are protected from twisting excessively.

Step into your skis and set the skis pointing in the same direction about a foot apart. The majority of skis will work on either foot but it is important to check and see if your skis have L or R markings on them, if so be sure to put them on the correct side. Stick your poles in the snow on each side of your skis. Hold onto your poles and then one foot at a time place the top of your boot into the flange at the heel and into the rear binding until you hear your boot click in place. Be sure to slide your feet back and forth a little to check the skis are attached and if not repeat the process again until they are both secure.

To take off your skis or reset them, push down on the lever that is found at the rear of your boot so that the boot is parallel to your skis. The easiest way to do this is to push the lever down using your pole. Should you have a fall and have difficulty righting yourself, remove the ski that is flat on the floor, get yourself balanced and together using the other ski and your poles, replace the ski that you have removed and you are ready to go again.

Learn the basics

One of the first things that you need to learn is how to move around on your skis. It is important that you know how to walk in skis as you will need to walk to the lift or if you are unfortunate and have a fall you may need to capture a wayward ski!

Probably the most common way to move yourself is to keep your skis parallel and push forward using your poles. Using both of your arms push the poles into the ground at a slight angle rearwards and rotate your arms backwards then repeat. Remember to pull one side more than the other to turn, make sure that you don't saw the skis backwards and forwards. This is the best way to get started on a downhill stretch as your skis are positioned parallel, ready to go.

There are a number of different ski techniques such as:

Herringbone – to complete a herringbone you need to make sure that the tips of your skis are pointing away from each, this will see you making a shape that looks like a big V, then you are ready to take little steps forwards. It is important that you also place the edge of the front ski into the snow slightly as you push forwards as this will prevent you from moving backwards. Lean forward and bend your knees and use the strong leg extension muscles to push yourself forward. You will need to spread your skis more the steeper the terrain and also if you find that you are slipping backwards. The poles are used to avoid you from slipping over and be sure to keep your poles on the outside of your skis so that you don't trip on them.

Another way to conquer an incline is by **side stepping**. Begin standing sideways to the slope, dig the uphill edges of your skis into the snow and make small steps sideways.

It is important that you find out which technique works for you, and be sure to remember that your legs muscles are stronger than your arms, this is particularly true of women and untrained men, and therefore as a beginner it is best to use the herringbone as much as possible to avoid tiring your upper body too quickly.

Do not attempt any uphill skiing until you are confident in all of the basic moves required for skiing.

For the beginners just starting to ski, it is important that they assume the basic skiing posture in the correct way. To do this they need to bend their knees and have their shins resting on the front of the boots and leaning forward slightly, there is no need to worry as the length of the skis will make it very unlikely for you to fall forwards. The person's hands should be through the straps on the ski poles and the polls by their side, whilst you probably won't use the poles they still need to be ready for you to use.

A beginner can stop themselves from sliding in any direction by assuming the herringbone position described above and if they find that they are sliding backwards, spread the back of the skis and this will stop them from sliding forwards. A beginner needs to know how to stop and to do so all they need to do is point the skis together whilst pointing their heels out so that they make the shape of a wedge with the open points and it is important that they do not overlap the tips of his skis as this will probably lead to a loss of control.

As well as stopping turning is also a vital part of skiing and in order to make a turn the beginner needs to point their feet and skis in the direction they want to travel, and if they need to stop whilst turning keep your feet in the snowplough position and turn across, this will bring you to a slow stop. If a beginner is in the position where they are about to crash they should not try to swerve as they will more than likely end up hitting something or someone else. Instead, fall to your side, and where possible fall uphill as doing so means that you are much less likely to get injured. Try to absorb a fall with your hip and shoulder and do not try to catch yourself with your arms as you are far more likely to injure your arm then you are your hip or shoulder.

Chairlift

When it is time to use a chairlift ski walk as discussed above up to the chairlift. If you have poles make sure that you take the straps of your wrists and safely hold both poles in one hand or under one arm. It is important that you take your poles off your wrists as this could be dangerous and make it far more challenging to get on the lift. Wait your turn and when the operator says you can go move quickly into the loading area, once there watch over your shoulder for the chair coming round. As the chair approaches grab the seat pole or back of the chair to steady yourself then sit down and let it pick you up. Lifts normally accommodate 2, 4 or 6 people per chair so be sure if your skiing with a friend that you are side by side when the chair approaches.

There is nothing stopping you from enjoying the view but do not lean over the edge of the chair whilst in the air for any reason. Leaning too far out of the lift could cause you to fall which will almost definitely result in a serious injury and could lead to death. As the chair reaches the top, point your skis forward and push away from the chair as it goes around, use the movement of the chair to push up and away from the lift. If for any reason you fail to get off the chairlift at the supposed point, don't panic and do not try to jump down. Stay put and someone will stop the lift and come and help you down.

Bunny Hill

Bunny Hill is the name given to a small incline that is usually equipped with a tow rope. This time of run is for beginners and they have the opportunity to get to grips with things including using a rope tow, chairlift or carpet lift all of which can be used to reach the top of the hill. The conveyor belt styled platform is more commonly referred to as a carpet lift and this belt is ideal for beginners, who need to begin by putting themselves forward onto the leading edge, ride the carpet lift which is similar to a large conveyor belt for most of the way with poles on the belt ready to brace on them and when you get to a few feet from the end lift your poles and lean gently forwards and ski smoothly to a halt at the end. If you're using a rope tow you need to grab hold of the handles when they come around and the rope will then pull you up the hill, don't push your heels in or resist and also sitting on the rope is not allowed. When you reach the top let go use the herring board to get away from the lift.

Once at the top of the Bunny Hill prepare yourself, be vigilant and watch for others, when clear begin sliding down the slope slowly. Keep your ski points together and when you reach the bottom, point your skis towards each other to make a wide-angle and this will stop you fairly quickly, in the event that you do fall be sure to point the skis so they point across the slope not down it, push yourself up and continue down the slope.

It is important to keep your weight in the correct place, if you lean too far back you will have a very hard time turning and this can even cause you to lose control and crash. Similarly, if you lean too far forward your skis will cross and you may wipe yourself out. The best technique is to keep your knees slightly bent and keep your hands in front of you like you're holding something out in front of you.

Conclusion

Now that you have reached the end of "How to Ski - Master the Basics of Skiing Quickly and Easily - The Ultimate Beginners Guide to Skiing," I do hope that you have found this book to be useful and informative.

Whether you are off on a skiing holiday in the near future or you just wanted an introduction before taking lessons I have attempted to cover all points that I believe a beginner would need to know.

Now that you have a basic grounding you are well on your way to becoming an accomplished skier and all that is left for me to do is thank you again for choosing this book and wish you the best as you venture into the start of your journey on the snow.

Good luck and enjoy!

13933923R00030

Printed in Great Britain
by Amazon.co.uk, Ltd.,
Marston Gate.